Baseboards
for
Model Railways

Ian Morton

Ian Allan
PUBLISHING

Title page: BR Standard Class 5 No 73051 crossing a small girder bridge on Tim Maddocks' Engine Wood layout. Scenery that falls below the track level is easier to create on an open-top baseboard than a solid-top one.
Photo: Tim Maddocks

First published 2007
Reprinted 2010

ISBN 978 0 7110 3153 1

Published by Ian Allan Publishing

an imprint of Ian Allan Publishing Ltd, Hersham Surrey KT12 4RG.

Printed by Ian Allan Printing Ltd, Hersham, Surrey KT12 4RG.

Visit the Ian Allan Publishing web site at:
www.ianallanpublishing.com

Right: An open-top baseboard before the scenic treatment has been applied. The railway is on an embankment above the roundabout. Open-top baseboards provide great flexibility when creating the model landscape and this can be as important in an urban setting as for a rural layout.

CONTENTS

Preface

Baseboards are not one of the most glamorous or enthralling aspects of railway modelling. At best they are regarded as a necessary evil, at worst something to be thrown together as quickly and cheaply as possible so that you can get on to the interesting stuff. Unfortunately the whole layout rests, literally, on your baseboard. If it develops warps and dips over time then your trains will run erratically. If the baseboard is unsuitable you will not be able to complete your layout.

I hope that this guide will take some of the mystery out of the black art of making baseboards. It covers various materials and techniques: some old, some new. By adopting a pick-and-mix approach you should be able to find something that fits both your skills and needs.

Before we start I should say something about measurements. On the whole I have used imperial measurements followed by their metric equivalent in brackets. It seems that many people still think in feet and inches so this is the line of least resistance. Hopefully, those of you who have been fully metricated will not find this an inconvenience.

In closing I should like to thank those who have provided photographs and information, and my family for tolerating the many hours that I spent putting this book together.

Happy modelling.

Ian Morton
March 2007

Introduction

Real railways know the importance of a good, firm foundation. Hardly surprising when you are running heavy trains. Whilst model railway trains are much lighter, a firm, level base will do a lot to ensure good running.
Photo: Author's collection

A model railway needs a structure to act as the bedrock of its scale world. This base, usually constructed of some form of wood, provides a firm and consistent base for the tracks and scenery as well as being somewhere to hang the various electrical items needed to make the trains move. Within these constraints this structure, normally called a baseboard, can be remarkably varied, not only in design but also material.

The baseboard is the very foundation of your model world. If it is well made and designed for the purpose it will easily outlast the layout that is built on top of it; if it is poorly made or inadequate then the layout will be continually beset by problems. There is little point in investing much time and effort in lovingly creating a miniature world if it is to be beset by earthquakes and subsidence.

Over the years virtually everything imaginable has been tried for use as a baseboard, from chipboard to ironing boards and from paste tables to poly-carbonate sheet. Some materials have stood the test of time; others have failed at the first hurdle. Some materials work better in certain conditions and there are a number of factors that you will need to bear in mind before finally deciding on which is best for you. Some materials need special techniques or tools to work them; others are too heavy to be moved easily. All have advantages and disadvantages, so careful consideration of your needs and options before you start will pay dividends later.

The first thing to consider is the type of layout that you want to build. Will it be permanent, movable or portable?

▪ A permanent layout is built into its location and cannot be extracted without dismantling or causing extensive damage.
The advantage is that you do not need to consider baseboard sizes or weight as you can build the supporting structure in one large piece.

The disadvantage is that if you wish to alter a section of the layout or move house then much, if not all, of the layout will need to be stripped down or destroyed.

- A movable layout is one that is designed so that it can be dismantled if necessary for modification or relocation. This may require cutting rails or wires at baseboard joins should a move be necessary but will not require large scale destruction. This is ideal for most people who have no desire to exhibit their layout but may need to move house.

It is also possible to replace one or more sections with new ones, to improve or extend the layout, without damaging the rest of the model railway.

- A portable layout is one that can be set up anywhere that there is room for it and moved to a different location with the minimum of inconvenience. This is ideal for those who wish to exhibit their layout or who move house frequently. It can also be a boon to the space-starved as the layout can be erected in a room for modelling or operation and then stored away at the end of the session.

Secondly, unless you are in the fortunate position of having someone else to build the baseboards for you, you need to consider your own skills, equipment and facilities. Cutting board and timber creates a lot of mess and noise. If you have to work in the evening in a room next to a sleeping child then carpentry will not be an acceptable option and you will need to select materials that can be worked more quietly. Similarly, unless you have your own table saw, or a helpful timber merchant, a baseboard that requires a large number of thin strips of plywood will be a time-consuming task compared to a conventional timber framed example. The ability to cut squarely and accurately is a necessary skill for many types of baseboard. If you are unable to do this, even with aids such as carpenter's squares and mitre boxes then a more permissive system, such as the L-girder, may be a better choice than a conventional solid-top baseboard.

Finding somewhere to build the baseboards can also present a problem. With long lengths of timber, large sheets of board and copious quantities of sawdust you need to find somewhere that can easily be kept clean, does not have much that can be easily damaged and will not inconvenience the rest of your family too

This portable layout was built on a solid-top baseboard. The canal basin was cut away to give a lower water level, and a retaining wall at the back supports some scenery at a higher level. As you can see, solid-top does not necessarily mean completely flat.
Photo: Neil Ripley

much. Ideally you don't want to have to put everything away and clear up every time you take a break, and don't even think of getting woodwork tools near laminate flooring: one carelessly dropped tool could cost you dearly.

If you have an area devoted to the layout, such as a spare bedroom, then this may seem like an ideal location. However, sometimes it is just not possible to assemble the baseboards in the area that they are intended to fit. As an example, to assemble a 4' × 2' (1.2m × 0.6m) baseboard you will need at least 7' × 4' (2.1m × 1.2m) of working area, assuming that your timber is no more than 6' (1.8m) long. You have also got to store the materials, tools and completed baseboards. Sometimes it is best to build the baseboards somewhere else, such as a garage, patio, driveway or even the kitchen (which is usually easier to clean than other rooms).

The layout's location will also play a part in your choice of materials. The attic of a well-insulated house will undergo large variations in temperature, whilst a typical cellar may well be damp. Both can cause havoc with the best constructed baseboard if it isn't suitable for its situation.

The layout's style needs to be considered. If your layout will be virtually all track on one level a solid-top baseboard will be ideal. If, on the other hand, you are considering a Welsh narrow-gauge line struggling up a towering mountain then an L-girder style baseboard would be a better option.

Finally, don't think that you need to use the same baseboard type for the whole layout. You could use solid-top for the main station, L-girder for the country section and a lightweight fully portable section for a branch terminus that you could take to exhibitions. Similarly, if you are extending or modifying an existing layout there is no law that states you must use the same type of baseboard as the rest of the layout. Experimenting with a different technique on a small section can be far less daunting than on a whole new layout.

When considering where to purchase the wood that is needed for most baseboards it is natural to think of the local DIY superstore as your first port of call. However, I would strongly advise checking your local timber yards or builders' merchants. Not only will they have a wider range and larger stock but they also tend to have more knowledgeable staff and cutting facilities. When purchasing the plywood for some of the baseboards built for this book the local branch of Jewson supplied me with an 8' × 4' (2.4m × 1.2m) sheet, cut into four 4' × 2' (1.2m × 0.6m) boards all for less than the DIY store a quarter of a mile away wanted for a single 4' × 2' (1.2m × 0.6m) sheet. It pays to shop around.

Solid-top baseboards can be used for scenes like this, Class 37 No 37424 at Peak Forest, as the line is at the bottom of the valley. Nonetheless an open-top baseboard could well make things easier when it comes to creating the tall hills in the background.
Photo: Author's collection

Former S&DJR 'Bulldog' 3F No 43218 starts away from Engine Wood with a local train for Templecombe on Tim Maddocks' layout. The embankment and overbridge add interest to what would otherwise be a flat scene.
Photo: Tim Maddocks

If you must have a flat layout then it is still possible to add some relief with tall trees or buildings to provide a backdrop. This is class 423/2 EMU No 3912 near Gatwick in 2000.
Photo: Author's collection

Constructing the baseboard is the model
equivalent of the civil engineering necessary
to build a real railway. No successful railway
was ever built on poor foundations. Whilst it
is tempting to rush the baseboards to get on
to the more exciting jobs, such as creating
scenes like this, shortcuts will come back to
haunt you in the forms of warping
baseboards and erratic running.
Photo: Author's collection

CHAPTER 2

Traditional Solid-top Baseboards

Solid-top baseboards are ideal if your layout has a lot of track, such as stations and goods yards. As this photograph shows, such locations can often be flat and level. They also make things easy if you frequently want to change things around.
Photo: Author's collection

Many a model railway has been built on a 'conventional' baseboard. In the model railway press this term is often used as convenient shorthand for a solid sheet material top on a timber frame. This has the advantage of being within the ability of anyone who is capable of sawing a piece of timber to length and requires few tools or planning. The solid top means that the baseboard can be constructed without needing to know where the track or other features will go and is ideal if your track is likely to be subject to frequent changes, such as on a child's layout. On the downside is the flatness of the resulting model world. Much effort needs to be expended to get changes in level. Another problem is the weight – the combination of the timber frame and solid top can make for very heavy units that often need two people to move them.

Traditionally the timber frame consists of 2" (50mm) × 1" (25mm) timber battens forming a grid of 12" (300mm) to 24" (600mm) squares. This should be 'prepared' timber which has been planed smooth and dried. The dimensions are nominal and may well be closer to 40mm × 20mm. If you get timber from two different sources it is not unusual for them to be slightly different sizes. If you do find yourself in this situation make sure that the top of the frame is all at the same level. The bottom of the frame is not as critical and the odd couple of millimetres don't make a great deal of difference here.

If you have deep point motors, other items that need to be hidden below the baseboard, or very heavy trains or scenery, you may choose to use a deeper frame of 3" (75mm) or even 4" (100mm) × 1" (25mm).

When buying timber you should check that it is straight and not warped or bowed. Similarly, it should be free from large knot holes as these affect the

The traditional baseboard is ideal for children's layouts that may be subjected to frequent changes of track plan and rough treatment. It is also good for the maximum track style of layout where there is little or no scenery. If the layout is firmly fixed in place then the weight of the baseboards will not tend to be a problem unless or until the layout needs to be moved or modified. Photo: Author's collection

timber's strength. If you buy your timber from the local DIY store then you may have to sort through their stock as much of it will fail these criteria. Much of the timber sold in DIY stores is not thoroughly dried and can warp with changes of humidity. It is best to buy kiln-dried timber; the extra expense will be worthwhile over the life of the baseboards.

There are a number of choices for the top surface.

Blockboard	Very hard and heavy. Hard to cut. Will not accept track pins unless you drill holes for them. Not recommended.
Chipboard	Easy to work but heavy. Will not accept track pins and needs special screws as ordinary screws can cause the material to break away. It is susceptible to damp conditions but can survive the occasional wetting, such as when ballasting track, without warping. It has been successfully used on both permanent and portable layouts, although for the latter you are advised to edge the baseboards with a strip of timber to protect the vulnerable edge of the chipboard.
Insulation board	This soft fibre board has very little strength and so needs closely spaced battens. It is also susceptible to damp. It is easy to drill but cutting it can leave a ragged edge. On the plus side you can push track pins in by hand.
MDF	This modern 'multi-purpose' material is one of the least suitable choices. It is heavy, very hard and resistant to pins. The dust can be harmful and so you are advised to wear a mask when drilling or cutting the board and be scrupulous when clearing up afterwards. It is also susceptible to

dampness and if you do use it you would be well advised to coat the finished boards with some form of varnish or sealant to avoid the possibility of warping caused by activities like ballasting the track.

Plywood

More expensive than MDF but superior in all respects. Depending on the scale of your models and scope of your scenery the thickness of the sheet can vary. Easy to cut and drill, it can accept track pins provided you push them in with a tool. Cheaper grades of plywood can splinter easily when being cut or drilled; the more expensive outdoor and marine grades are recommended for baseboard construction. When the baseboard is complete a coat of varnish will stop any dampness getting into the boards and also help to stop any splintering on the edges.

Sundeala

This dense 9mm thick board made from recycled newspaper is easy to cut and drill, accepts track pins and, as a bonus, absorbs some of the noise from moving trains. It is supplied in 1200mm × 600mm (47$\frac{1}{4}$" × 23$\frac{3}{4}$") sheets. This material can be difficult to locate as it is not widely stocked. Some model shops can supply it. Alternatively you can contact the manufacturer to locate a local supplier. (Sundeala Limited, Middle Mill, Cam, Dursley, GL11 5LQ. Email: sales@sundeala.co.uk. Tel: 01453 540900. Web: www.sundeala.co.uk)

Your timber supplier may be able to supply your board in suitable sizes for your baseboards, such as 3' (90cm) × 2' (60cm), 4' (120cm) × 2' (60 cm) or be willing to cut larger boards down to size for you. If using pre-cut boards it is advisable to check that they are square and all the same size. Correcting any such problems before construction starts will be much easier than trying to rectify them later.

If you have to cut the boards to size yourself then you will probably need to use either a circular saw or a jigsaw. Ensure that you have the board supported on a suitable work surface, such as a pair of Black & Decker Workmates, to avoid the possibility of the board slipping whilst you are cutting. Not only would this ruin your baseboard but, more importantly, could lead to injury.

Tools

- Drill. Used to make pilot holes for screws. I used a hand drill but an electric one would be equally good.
- Screwdriver. Choose one that is the correct size and type for the screws that you will be using.
- Carpenter's square
- Pencil
- Claw hammer, for knocking in panel pins (and pulling them out if necessary)
- $\frac{3}{4}$" (19mm) chisel
- Mallet, for chiselling
- Knife
- Metal ruler or tape measure
- Electric jigsaw or hand saw
- Safety goggles if using electric tools
- Workbench (such as a Black & Decker Workmate)

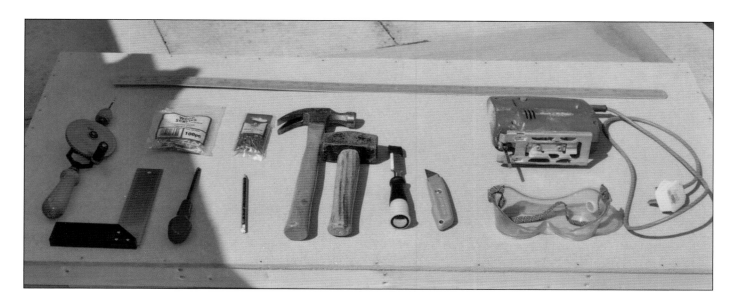

Building the Baseboard

For this example I will build a 4' (120cm) × 2' (60cm) baseboard with a Sundeala board top. This would be an ideal starter board for an 'N' scale layout or three could be joined together to make a 6' (180cm) × 4' (120cm) layout as a permanent home for an 'OO' train set.

Materials

- Sundeala Hobbyboard – 1 sheet 47$\frac{1}{4}$" × 23$\frac{3}{4}$" (1200mm × 600mm)
- 2" × 1" (44mm × 18mm)* PSE timber – 3 lengths 2.1m long
- 1" × 1" (21mm × 21mm)* PSE timber – 1 length 2.1m long
- 25 No 6 screws – 1$\frac{1}{2}$" (40mm) long
- About 50 panel pins 1" (25mm) long
- Woodworking glue

* All timber sizes are approximate and will vary from supplier to supplier.

Assembly

1. The Sundeala needs to be conditioned before use. Mix a drop of washing up liquid to half a litre of water for each sheet that you are going to use. Mop the water on the rear (printed) side of each board. Place the boards flat on the floor, wet side to wet side, in the room where they are to be used and leave them for 48 to 72 hours. You may wish to weight the boards down to ensure that they stay flat. This process will ensure that the boards do not absorb moisture from the atmosphere and expand whilst you are building with them.

2. Check that the Sundeala board is square. Check the length and width. Correct if necessary. Check one end of each length of 2" × 1" (44mm × 18mm) timber is square. If not, cut it square. Mark the other end. The marked end should NOT be used for measuring and cutting. It is important that all the cuts you make in the timber are square and that when you join two pieces of timber the join is both square and level; otherwise your frame will be out of true and may distort the surface of the board.

3. Cut two lengths of 2″ × 1″ (44m × 18mm) timber to the same length as the Sundeala board (47¼″/1200mm). These will be the two long sides of the frame.

4. Subtract the thickness of two lengths of timber (about 1½″/36mm) from the width of the Sundeala board (23¾″/600mm). Cut five pieces of timber to this length (22¼″/564mm). These will be the short sides of the frame and the cross-members.

5. Make sure that the timber is firmly held so that it doesn't move whilst you are cutting it. When using an electric jigsaw safety goggles are a necessity to avoid getting any sawdust or splinters in your eyes.

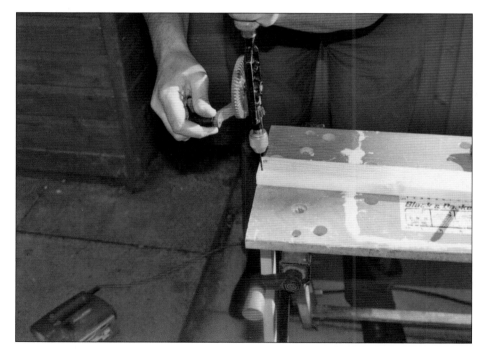

6. Place one of the long lengths of timber in the workbench. Place one of the short pieces to form an 'L' as shown above. Drill pilot holes for two screws. Apply some glue to the join and then screw the two pieces together.

7.   Check that the 'L' is square and adjust if necessary before the glue dries.

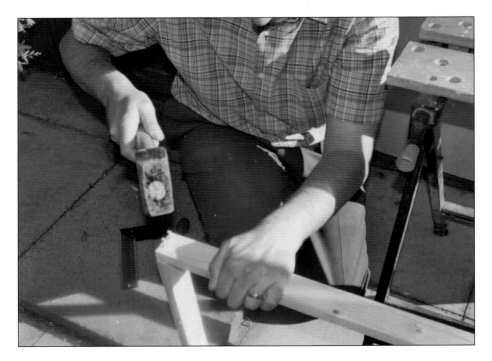

8.   Repeat with the other two identical pieces. You may find it useful to drive
      the screws in until their points just project from the underside of the side
      members, line the timbers up and then tap the screws with a mallet to mark
      their location on the cross-member.

9.   Using the same process join the two 'L' pieces to make a rectangle.

10. Having checked that the frame is square you can now measure the centre beam and cut it to length. To simplify the carpentry work, this is made from 1″ × 1″ (21mm × 21mm) timber.

11.   The cross-members need to be notched to fit over the centre beam. First measure in about 10 ³/₄" (270mm) from one end and mark one edge of the notch. Also mark the end that you measured from so that you can position the cross-members the right way round.

12.   Use a piece of 1" × 1" (21mm × 21mm) timber to mark the width and depth of the slot.

13. Clearly mark the area that is to be removed to avoid mistakes when cutting out.

14. Saw along both sides of the notch. Cut along the inside of the pencil lines.

15. Using the chisel knock out the waste piece. The notch can then be cleaned up, if necessary, with the knife.

16. The centre beam can be screwed and glued in position and then the cross-members can be put in place.

17. The cross-members are attached with two screws through the side members at each end and one screw into the centre beam.

18. Turn the frame over and nail the Sundeala board in place using the panel pins. Nailing the board to the centre beam and cross-members as well as the outer frame will minimise any possibility of bumps and hollows developing.

19.   The completed board shown from underneath. Although I have not done it
       on the demonstration board, you may wish to drill a number of holes in the
       cross-members for wires to pass through.

The Sundeala board is easy to drill and accepts track pins and screws easily,
making it an ideal surface for a layout that is likely to see regular changes.
    The large amount of cross bracing used on the demonstration baseboard
could be reduced but this would increase the probability of the surface developing hollows over time. An alternative would be to use sturdier material for the
top, such as plywood.

Traditional solid-top baseboards	
Advantages	**Disadvantages**
Easy to build.	Heavy.
You don't need to know where everything is going to go before you build the baseboard.	Scenery has a tendency to appear flat and unrealistic.
Easy to change the layout once built.	Difficult to build multi-level layouts.
Will stand up to a lot of use.	

Adding an Extra Level to a
Solid-top Baseboard

If you need more trackage in a congested area then you can always go upwards, just like the real railways do. This is Class 47 47049 at Tay Bridge, Dundee in 1985. As well as adding extra trackage, elevated tracks like these give great views of your trains in action.
Photo: Author's collection

Many model railways make use of an extra level to increase the amount of track that can be squeezed into the limited space that most of us have at our disposal. Typically this will involve a high level station situated over a running line or storage loops. A second level can easily be added to a solid-top base-board. Whilst this does not give the flexibility of an open-frame baseboard it does enable a flat layout to be remodelled or extended without having to scrap everything to start again.

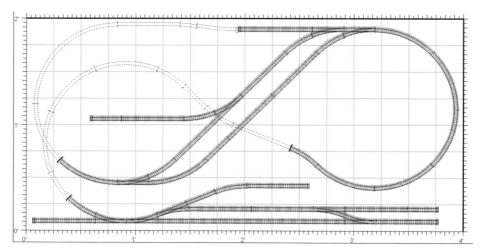

The complete track plan for the single board 'N' or 'OO9' layout. No scenic treatment has been indicated, but a mountainous area would best match the overall design. It would be good as a South Wales coal branch in 'N' or a North Wales slate line in 'OO9'.

For the example baseboard in this section I shall start with a plywood-topped baseboard built in the same manner as in the previous chapter. The overall dimensions are 120cm × 60cm, which is a little under 4'x 2'. I have designed this as an 'N' scale layout on a single board, but it would be equally at home as an 'OO9' narrow-gauge project provided that you checked the clearances.

A terminus station, at the front of the layout, represents a wharf. This is at the lowest level. The track runs into a tunnel, turns and runs back across the board. After it emerges from the tunnel it starts to climb around another curve. At the top of the gradient the line levels out and the train can either run into the upper station or around a reverse loop and into the station from the other end. The station has a loading siding for a mine or quarry and a run around or passing loop. The reverse loop is hidden in another tunnel and both the upper station and the reverse loop are above the main line on the lower level.

The lower level lines are shown in orange. These would be laid directly on the baseboard top. The pink line is the gradient that climbs to the upper level.

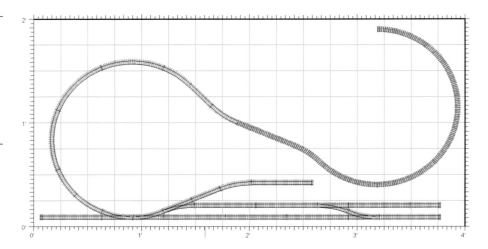

The low level tracks are shown above, with the gradient highlighted in pink. The front track is the transhipment line. The siding to the left is for a loco spur or engine shed. The rear siding could store extra stock and passenger facilities could be provided on the centre line.

This shows the high level tracks with the station and reverse loop. The tracks will be laid on a separate baseboard.

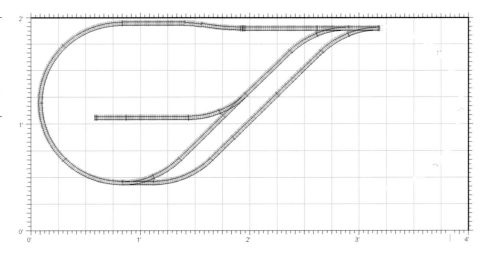

The high level tracks will be on a separate baseboard and consist of the high level station and the reverse loop. These will all be level, the only gradient being the highlighted section of the low level plan.

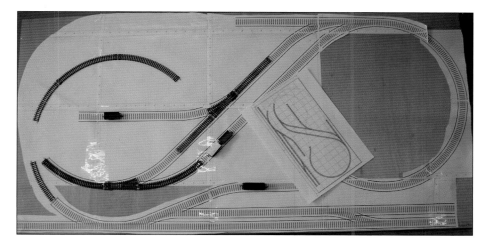

With a solid-top baseboard you can check your track plan before you start to build. Here a full-size track plan has been laid on the baseboard along with a few pieces of track and rolling stock to establish the overall effect. This did lead to some small changes prior to construction.

One advantage of a solid-top baseboard is that you can use it to test your track plan and see if any changes need to be made. This is really useful if you are trying to squeeze a lot into a small space or cannot visualise how the layout will appear from your plan.

The next step was to mark out the section of baseboard that would become the gradient. This needs to be a continuous strip wide enough to accommodate the track with space on either side.

Cutting the gradient section from the baseboard top. Do not cut this strip away at the bottom end of the gradient, only the sides and top. Here the metal rule is acting as a marker for the position of the next cross-member that will be encountered.

Once the gradient had been marked out (and checked, twice) a jigsaw was used to cut through the baseboard on either side of the strip. You need to take care not to cut through the baseboard cross-members when doing this. You will end up with a number of cuts interspersed with short lengths of uncut wood where the baseboard crosses the supporting structure. Only cut along the sides and top end of the gradient section, not the bottom end – you need to leave this attached to the rest of the baseboard surface.

The knife that was used to join the cuts in the plywood gradient strip that were made with the jigsaw.

The cuts can now be joined by cutting through the plywood with a knife. Don't try to do this with one stroke. Repeated gentle passes with the knife will give a cleaner cut and be far easier on your wrist.

The gradient strip has now been cut out and raised on scraps of timber to check the overall height and effect. An 'N' gauge diesel shunter is on a length of track under the highest section to check the clearances for the hidden trackage.

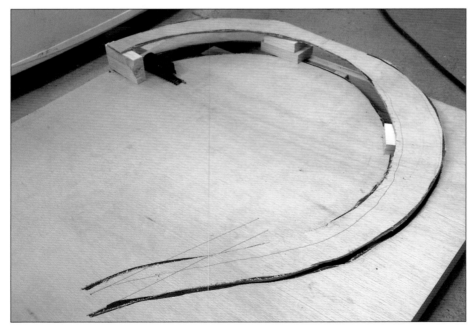

Once the entire strip has been cut it is possible to get an idea of the gradient by packing it up with scrap pieces of timber.

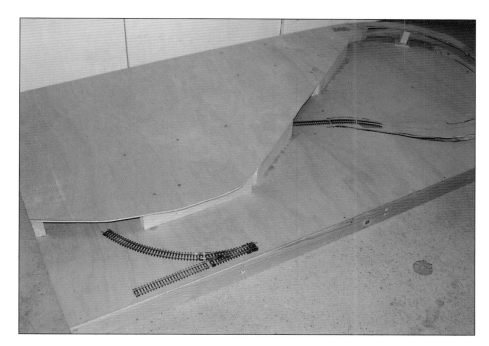

The top level baseboard has now been cut from a sheet of plywood and put on more odd lengths of timber to check its size and shape.

The top level can now be cut from another sheet of ply. As this layout is in 'N' scale, lengths of 2" (44mm) wide timber will provide sufficient headroom. For larger scales you have the choice of using wider timber or making another full baseboard that stands on its own short legs.

Access holes have been cut in the baseboard so that any trains that get into difficulties on the hidden track can be rescued. 2" × 1" (44mm × 18mm) timber on its side has been glued in place to support the upper level.

Once the upper baseboard is in position the track in the lower level tunnel will be completely inaccessible unless provision is made to get at any trains that come to grief. On this baseboard two access holes were cut in the board, either side of a cross-member, and a gap was left in the upper level supports at the back of the layout. This will enable limited access to the track in emergencies without having to remove the upper level.

Another view of the upper level supports and access arrangements for the hidden trackage. This is an area where advance planning is needed: it would be difficult to retrieve a derailed train if the area was completely enclosed.

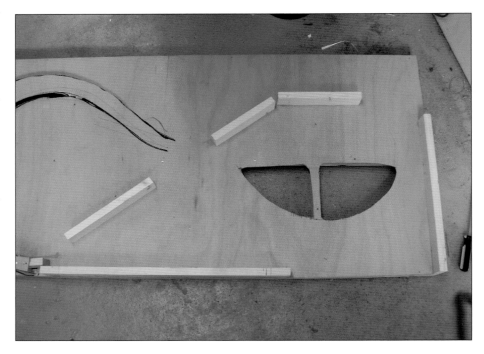

As this is an 'N' gauge layout 44mm × 18mm timber on its side gives sufficient clearance for the low level track. For '00' it might be necessary to allow more headroom; it depends on the design of the stock that you will be using. Some lengths were glued to the lower baseboard to support the upper level. A gap was left at the back to provide additional access to the hidden tracks.

The top baseboard seen from underneath. The long beams are for support whilst the short ones are to locate the board in position.

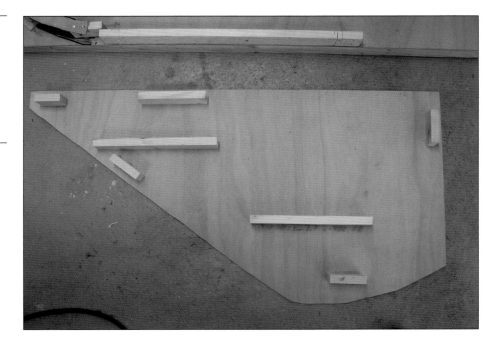

Other lengths of timber were glued to the underside of the top level. Two long pieces provide additional support whilst shorter pieces fit behind the pieces fixed to the lower section to hold the board in the correct position.

The top baseboard is secured in place with screws that pass through the supports glued to the lower baseboard and then into the short supports glued to the upper level.

Screws through the outer and inner supports hold the top in place. If the baseboard is to be stored on its side then you may also wish to secure the front of the top board using a screw from beneath the lower board into one of the supports.

This is the view from the back, showing the gap that gives access to the hidden tracks.

This is the gradient showing where the plywood has been cut away from the solid top to make a gradient. It is supported by wooden risers.
The first is attached to a cross-member; the second to the baseboard end; the third is seated on a plywood cross piece that bridges the gap left in the baseboard top whilst the final riser is attached to the baseboard surface.

The completed baseboard is seen from above. Access to the hidden low level track is from the rear and beneath. On the upper level the rear of the loop will be hidden by scenery and suitable access will need to be arranged.
The layout could be extended in a number of ways. At the lower level the sidings at the front could be extended to the left or right onto a new baseboard. Alternatively an extra point on the upper level could provide a line running onto a new baseboard to the left.

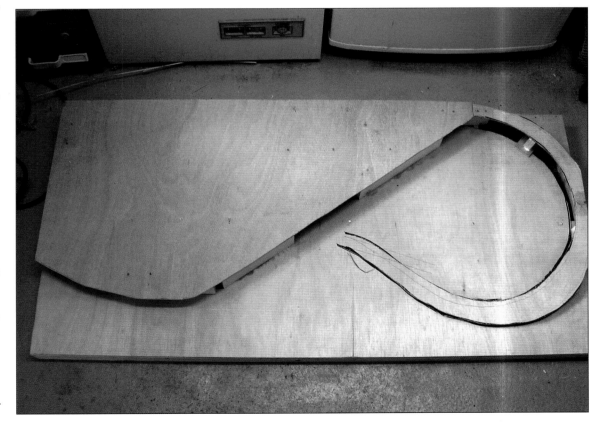

A bridge over a river valley is almost a modelling cliché, but when well executed still makes a very appealing scene.
Photo: Author's collection

Another common feature that is popular on layouts is a bridge carrying the railway over a road, river or canal. Such a scene can be included on a layout using solid-top baseboards, provided that you plan for it in advance.

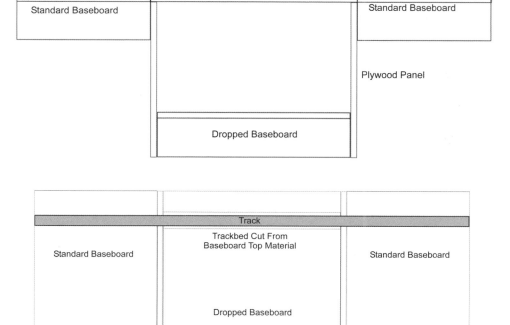

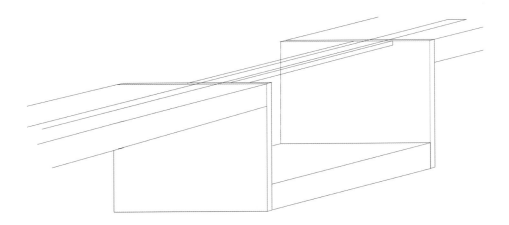

Once you have decided where the bridge will be you need to make a lowered section of baseboard. This is made in exactly the same way as a normal baseboard but instead of being joined on the same level as the baseboards on either side is fixed to a plywood panel at each end. These panels are then fixed to the adjacent baseboards giving a drop equivalent to the height of the panels. The track can be built onto a section of baseboard top cut to suit and supported on piers of timber, the model bridge or a combination of both. Of course, to make the most of the scenic potential you might like to consider using an open-top baseboard for the dropped section.

BR Standard Class 4 No 75023 arrives at Engine Wood station with a Bristol Temple Meads – Bournemouth train. This section of the Somerset & Dorset was modelled by Tim Maddocks.
Photo: Tim Maddocks

Open-top Baseboards

An open-top baseboard before the scenery has been added. This will be part of an urban scene with the railway on an embankment running through a town centre. Here the line crosses a road on a girder bridge.
Photo: Author's collection

Open-top is a term that covers a number of different types of baseboard. Their common factor is that there is no surface covering the whole of the base-board frame. Instead the surface material is cut to the shape of the roadbed and associated areas. By raising the roadbed on some form of support the lineside scenery can rise and fall as needed.

Whilst the open-top system does give you a great deal of flexibility it does impose the need to plan in advance. Unlike a solid-top baseboard you cannot make large changes to the track layout without revising the baseboard. As a result the open-top system is often seen as the preserve of the more advanced modeller. This need not be true, anymore than the idea that the solid-top base-board is only suitable for beginners. The open- and solid-top baseboards can be mixed together in the same layout without any problem or penalty.

Open-top baseboard construction allows subtle variations in ground level to be constructed with ease.
This view of Tim Maddocks' Bleakhouse Road under construction shows various levels.
Photo: Tim Maddocks

Many people who build layouts set in towns or cities feel that the solid-top baseboard is best suited to this type of model, with open-top baseboards being applicable only to lines in open countryside. This is, of course, nonsense. Just because an area has been built on doesn't mean that it is also flat. Railways through towns and cities often find themselves on embankments and in cuttings.

Grid

The simplest open-top baseboard is the grid design. This is just like the baseboard frame for a traditional solid-top baseboard (see chapter 2) but without the surface attached. The cross members need to be spaced about 16" (40.5cm) to 18" (45.5cm) apart so that you have room to drill holes and drive screws in. The cross members need to be 2" (50mm) deep rather than the 1" (25mm) used in chapter 2 in order to make it easier to attach the risers that will hold the roadbed.

The sub-roadbed is held in place by a 1" × 1" (25mm × 25mm) cleat that attaches to the riser. The riser is, in turn, screwed to the baseboard cross members so that the track is supported at the correct height.

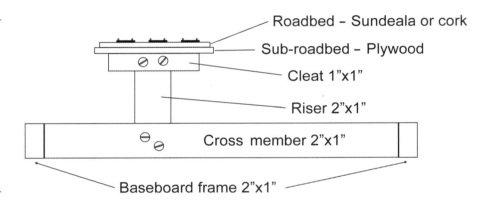

The risers should be made from 2" × 1" (50mm × 25mm) timber attached by two screws to the cross members. At the top a 1" (25mm) square section of timber acts as a cleat to which the roadbed, typically plywood, is attached. The roadbed should not be screwed directly to the cross members, even on the lowest track level. If you do this you will find it exceedingly difficult to fit the risers where the track needs to climb. Instead a cleat needs to be fitted, despite appearing to be a waste of timber.

The first step in constructing a grid-type open-top baseboard is to construct the grid itself. This is then fitted to the legs and erected. The sections of roadbed then need to be cut out. You may find it beneficial to lay the uncut sheets of plywood on the grid. You can then test the fit of the trackage and other features before taking a saw to them. Once you have marked out the plywood it can be transferred to the workbench and the roadbed cut out with a jigsaw. The resulting pieces can then be returned to the grid for a final check.

The risers need to be cut to approximately the correct length before being screwed in place. The length can be calculated as:

Desired track height minus roadbed thickness minus height of the bottom of the grid above the floor.
For example:

Desired track height = 46" (1.17m)

Roadbed thickness = ³/₄" (1.9cm)

Height of bottom of grid above floor = 36" (91.2cm)

Riser length = 46 – ³/₄ – 36 = 9¹/₄" (23.1cm)

Two grid-style baseboards made from a mixture of ply girders and foamcore cross members for an urban layout. A roadway has been attached directly to the baseboard. The plywood roadbed has been cut to shape and is now ready for the risers to be fitted.
Photo: Author's collection

If in doubt always cut the riser longer than you need. If the riser is too short you won't be able to fix it in place properly.

Then the cleat, a piece of timber the same length as the roadbed width, is screwed across one end of the riser. This end will be the top. The completed riser is then clamped to the appropriate place on the cross member. Once a few risers have been positioned then the roadbed can be laid back in place and the risers adjusted to give proper support. Always use a spirit level to check that the roadbed is level in both the horizontal and vertical planes, except where you want it to be on a gradient. It is very easy to end up with unintentional slopes. The risers can then be attached to the cross-member by drilling pilot holes and screwing them in place. After this you can trim any excess that extends below the cross member.

The roadbed is then fixed to the cleats, again by drilling pilot holes and screwing it in place. Ideally this too should be done from underneath to retain the maximum amount of flexibility but, in practice, many people prefer the ease of screwing downward through the roadbed and into the cleat.

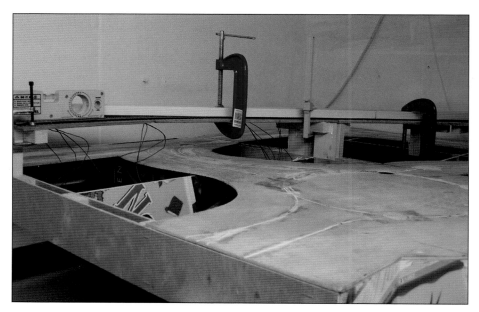

Fitting the risers and roadbed needs a good selection of clamps to hold things together whilst you drill and screw.
The length of timber was used to protect the track that had been laid in advance of fitting the roadbed.
Always use a spirit level to check that the track that is supposed to be level is level, both along and across the roadbed.
Photo: Author's collection

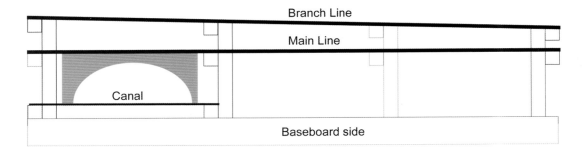

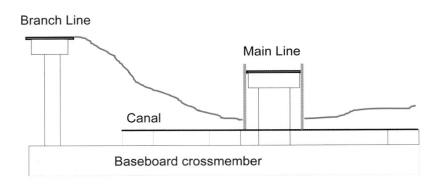

Frame

The frame design is more complex and needs more advance planning than the grid system. Instead of the normal cross members, shaped profile pieces, usually of plywood, are used. These provide support for the scenic shell as well as the roadbed. This results in a sturdy, though heavy, baseboard best suited to permanent layouts. Indeed it is commonly used on model railways that are open to the public as a commercial business. The frame design uses large quantities of wood and so is unsuited to a portable layout unless a lightweight substitute such as foamcore board is utilised.

There are two commonly used types of frame baseboards. In the first instead of the cross members being a piece of timber with risers to support the track each cross member is replaced by a profile which is a cross-section of the scenery at that point. Flat sections are left for the roadbed, which is attached to the profiles by timber cleats. Where tracks run in tunnels a hole must be cut in the profile piece. The profiles provide basic contours for the scenery and help to support the scenic landscape.

Front and, if necessary, rear facia boards are used to help retain the profiles in position. The combination of roadbed and facia boards is normally sufficient to avoid the need for extra bracing between the profile boards. The second style of frame baseboard uses profile sections attached to a grid-style baseboard. You can, of course, combine the two types in the same layout, using the grid-type of baseboard for flatter areas and the frame-type for the hillier sections.

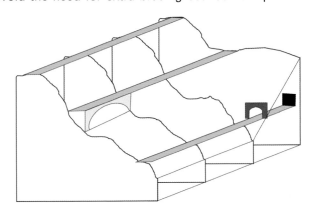

L-girder Baseboards

John Allen's Gorre & Daphetid Railroad is a classic example of using open-top baseboards to the limit. This famous model railway filled the basement of John Allen's home and had scenery that ran literally from floor to ceiling. Many US layouts use mountainous scenery and multi-level tracks which require a flexible baseboard system.
Photo: Author's collection

Linn Westcott, in his time as editor of the American *Model Railroader* magazine, is widely credited with inventing L-girder baseboards in the early 1960s. As originally conceived, the system used sturdy timbers to support the US-style layout with large plaster-covered mountains through which tracks were threaded on many levels. Naturally these were permanent layouts that were never moved, but none the less the system was remarkably flexible, allowing the baseboards to be revised and remodelled should the builder wish to change or replace a section of the model railway. The system has proved itself over the years, able to support heavy multi-level scenery over long periods of time whilst able to be erected or altered quickly and easily. For a long-term medium to large project the L-girder has a lot to commend it.

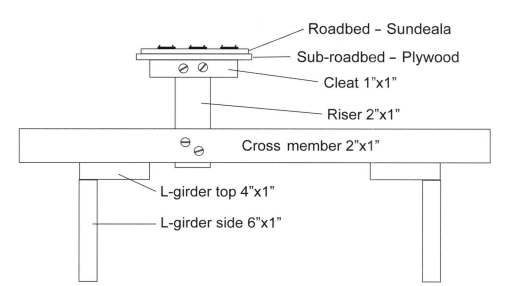

Roadbed – Sundeala
Sub-roadbed – Plywood
Cleat 1"x1"
Riser 2"x1"
Cross member 2"x1"
L-girder top 4"x1"
L-girder side 6"x1"

This diagram shows the components of an L-girder baseboard. The two L-girders provide the basic structure to which the cross-members and risers are added to support the roadbed.

The key to the design was a pair of 'L'-shaped wooden girders that ran along the length of the baseboard. Typically each girder is constructed from a 6" × 1" (15cm × 2.5cm) vertical section topped with a 4" × 1" (10cm × 2.5cm) horizontal piece. 2" × 1" (5cm × 2.5cm) cross-members run across the girders with risers to raise the track to the required level. The track is laid on a Sundeala roadbed supported by plywood which is attached to the risers using 1" × 1" (2.5cm × 2.5cm) cleats. All the joins are made with screws so that any of the pieces can be moved or removed. This is the key to the L-girder's flexibility as any of the cross-members can be moved, either temporarily to give access, or permanently to clear a point motor, at any time during the construction process.

The cross-members can be of varying length to allow the edge of the layout to move in or out to gain space in aisles or for scenic features. They can also be positioned diagonally to support curved tracks, clear obstructions or provide access. The L-girder system makes it easy to have a free-flowing layout edge instead of the dead-straight edges more common on layouts built in the UK. Normally a facia board of thin ply or hardboard is screwed to the ends of the cross-members to make a defined layout edge.

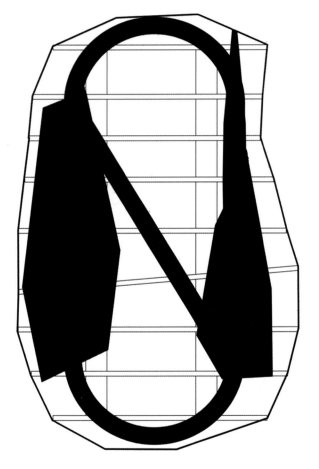

Viewed from above the ability of the L-girder system to follow the layout's outline is evident. The roadbed (shown in black) is supported on cross-members of varying lengths which rest on the L-girders that run the length of the layout. A facia board runs around the layout, matching the overall shape to the layout's plan and scenic treatment.

The full specification L-girder uses a lot of timber and, whilst it can support the proverbial elephant, tends to be over-specified for the average UK layout. Whilst the layout can be freeform rather than constricted by the baseboard shape, construction is complex, and in areas where there is restricted clearance the need for about a foot (30cm) of baseboard structure between track level and the bottom of the girders can cause problems. If your lowest track is 3' (91cm) above the floor then the bottom of the L-girders would be around 2' (60cm) above the floor, a point that is often overlooked until you come to wire the layout and which would lead to great discomfort.

Fortunately for most layouts far less substantial timbers can be used without losing the structural benefits. Typically a 3" × 1" (7.5cm × 2.5cm) or even a 2" × 1" (5cm × 2.5cm) upright and 2" × 1" (5cm × 2.5cm) top will provide adequate support. The cross-members still need to support the weight of the roadbed and scenery so there is only limited scope for reducing their size. In addition there must be sufficient space available to secure the risers with two screws both at the cleat and cross-member which means that a 1½" × 1" (3.7cm × 2.5cm) cross-member is probably the smallest practicable size.

The cross-members should be spaced about 16" (40.5cm) to 18" (45.5cm) apart – you don't want them too close or you won't be able to drill holes or drive screws in. If they are spaced too far apart then the roadbed will not have sufficient support and will sag over time. Using thicker plywood (for example ½" (12mm) ply instead of ⅜" (9mm) will enable you to increase the gap between the risers.

Making L-girders

The L-girders are the primary load-bearing component and need to be constructed carefully.

One option, if you have a circular saw and a saw table is to cut a larger piece of timber to suit. For example, a 4" × 2" (10cm × 5cm) length of timber could have a 3" × 1" (7.5cm × 2.5cm) strip cut out along one side giving you a 4" (10cm) tall, 2" (5cm) wide L-girder and a length of 3" × 1" (7.5cm × 2.5cm) timber to use for legs or cross-members.

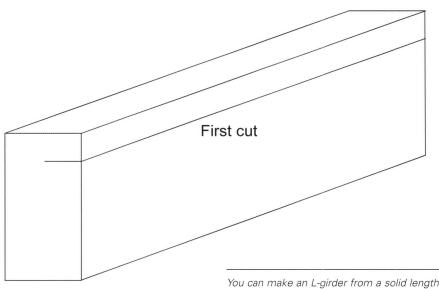

First cut

You can make an L-girder from a solid length of timber if you have access to a circular saw mounted in a saw table.
Starting with a 4" × 2" (100mm × 50mm) piece of timber you make a cut 1" (25mm) deep and 1" (25mm) in on one of the long sides.

The second cut is made cut 1″ (25mm) deep and 1″ (25mm) in the short side as shown.

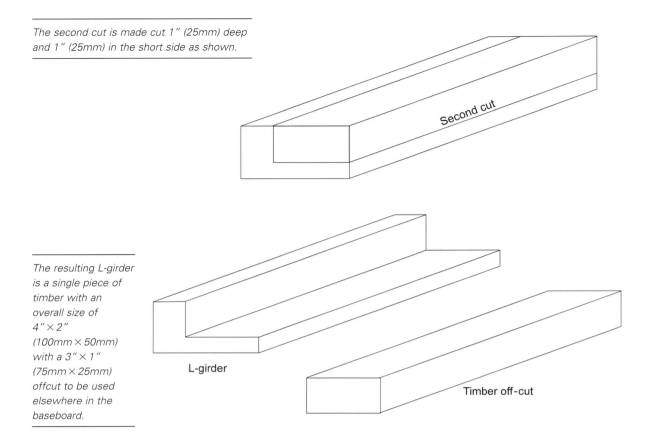

Second cut

The resulting L-girder is a single piece of timber with an overall size of 4″ × 2″ (100mm × 50mm) with a 3″ × 1″ (75mm × 25mm) offcut to be used elsewhere in the baseboard.

L-girder

Timber off-cut

If you do not have the facilities to create the L-girder by cutting then you need to join two lengths of timber together to form the 'L' shape. The lengths of timber need to be both flat and straight and with as few knot holes as possible. It is worth getting high-quality kiln-dried wood from your local timber yard as well made L-girders can last you for several layouts.

L-girders can easily be constructed by joining two lengths of timber together. Careful selection of the lengths of timber used will be of benefit both in the construction and in the longevity of the girders.
Use the best quality timber that you can find. Check that it has few knot holes and is straight in both the horizontal and the vertical planes.
Photo: Author's collection

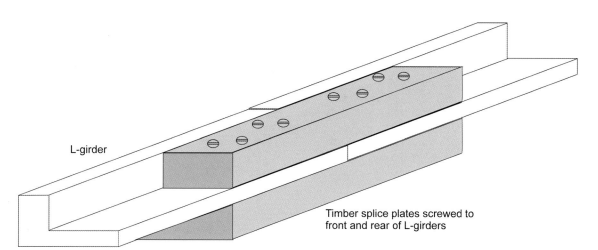

L-girder

Timber splice plates screwed to
front and rear of L-girders

*Scrap timber can be
used to join lengths
of L-girder together
to make long girders
to run the length of
your layout.*

The top length needs to be glued and nailed or screwed to the bottom one.
Spread glue along the top of the vertical timber. Place the top section on, resting
the other side on some spare timber. Nail the top section in place at one end and
then work along, nailing or screwing it in place every 18" (45.5cm) or so – taking
care to keep the two parts in alignment all the way. When you have finished wipe
away any glue that has been squeezed out, using a damp cloth.

You can join shorter lengths of L-girder together to suit the length of your
layout by making splice plates from lengths of timber and screwing them in
place. It is a good idea to have legs close to either side of the splice to minimise
any tendency for the joint to flex.

It is also possible to depart from the normal parallel configuration to accommodate odd shapes or locations. For example, in a situation where a terminus
connects to a continuous run you may have a narrow baseboard for the station
and a wide baseboard for the rest of the layout. The two sections could share one
long L-girder along one side with two shorter girders on the other side, to suit the
lengths of each section.

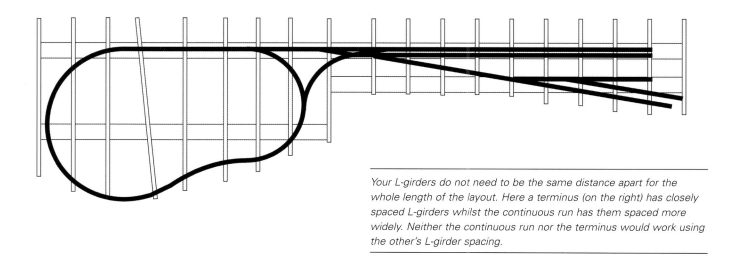

*Your L-girders do not need to be the same distance apart for the
whole length of the layout. Here a terminus (on the right) has closely
spaced L-girders whilst the continuous run has them spaced more
widely. Neither the continuous run nor the terminus would work using
the other's L-girder spacing.*

Attaching Legs

Legs can be made from any suitable size of timber. The top of each leg is screwed to the outside of the 'L'. Diagonal braces from thin timber can be run up to a spacer attached to the L-girder or the next leg. Normally the legs will be braced both parallel and at right-angles to the L-girders. Where the layout runs along a wall one of the L-girders can be fixed directly to the wall.

It is normal for the L-girders to face outward for ease of access when fixing the cross-members. The main exception to this is where an L-girder is fixed to a wall in which case it needs to face out from the wall.

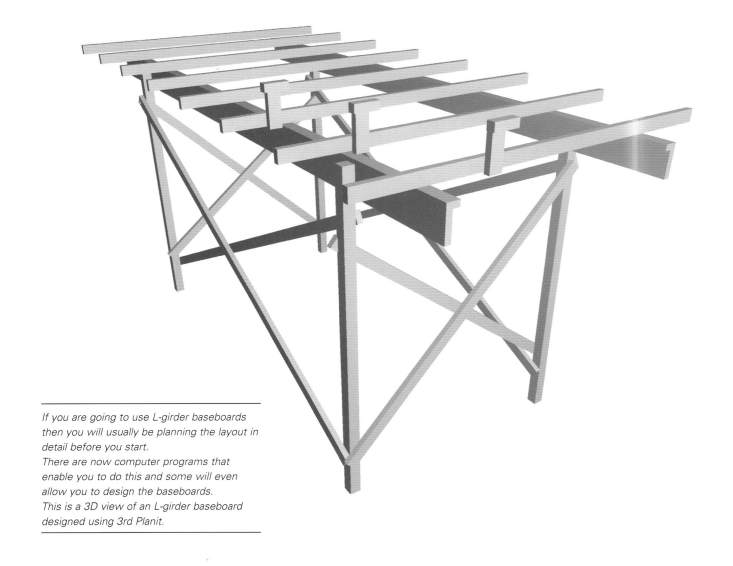

If you are going to use L-girder baseboards then you will usually be planning the layout in detail before you start.
There are now computer programs that enable you to do this and some will even allow you to design the baseboards.
This is a 3D view of an L-girder baseboard designed using 3rd Planit.

Cross-members

The cross-members are screwed to the top of the L-girder. The screw should go up, through the top of the 'L' and into the cross-member. This enables the screws to be taken out and the cross-member moved or removed in the future. You will need to hold the cross-member in place with a G-clamp whilst you drill a pilot hole and put the screw in. Obviously the screw should be shorter than the thickness of the top of the 'L' and the height of the cross-member added together. For a 1" (2.5cm) thick girder section and a 2" (5cm) tall cross-member a 1½" (3.7cm) long screw will be ideal.

Roadbed

The next stage is to cut the roadbed to shape from plywood sheet. This can be done with a jigsaw on a workbench. You can position the pieces on the cross-members as you cut them to check their shape and fit. It is best to make any small adjustments to the roadbed and cross-member positions at this point. Once you are happy with the roadbed you can take it off the cross-members and turn your attention to the risers.

Risers and Cleats

Risers are screwed to the cross-members using two screws. If you use only one screw then they are able to rotate and, as a result, cause havoc with the trackbed. Assuming a 1" (2.5cm) thick cross-member and riser then you can use the same 1½" (3.7cm) long screws used to secure the cross-members to the L-girders.

The risers need to be cut to approximately the correct length before being screwed in place. The length can be calculated as:

> Desired track height minus roadbed thickness minus height of top of L-girder above the floor
>
> For example:
> Desired track height = 46" (1.17m)
> Roadbed thickness = ½" (1.3cm)
> Height of top of L-girder above floor = 36" (91.2cm)
> Riser length = 46 – ½ – 36 = 9½" (24.5cm)

If in doubt always cut the riser longer than you need. If the riser is too short you won't be able to fix it in place properly.

Then the cleat, a piece of timber the same length as the roadbed width, is screwed across one end of the riser. This end will be the top. If two pieces of roadbed are to join over a riser then it might be advisable to fit a second piece of timber across the other side at the top for the second section of roadbed to be fastened to.

The completed riser is then clamped to the appropriate place on the cross-member. Since the riser's height will need to be adjusted slightly when the roadbed is fitted, it should not be permanently fixed to start with. Once a number of risers have been positioned then the roadbed can be laid back in place and the risers adjusted to give proper support. The risers can then be attached to the cross-member by drilling pilot holes and screwing them in place. Do not be tempted to glue the risers to the cross-member as this will prevent you from dismantling them in the future should you wish to move or remove them.

The roadbed is then fixed to the cleats, again by drilling pilot holes and screwing it in place. Ideally this too should be done from underneath to retain the maximum amount of flexibility but, in practice, many people prefer the ease of screwing downward through the roadbed and into the cleat.

Finishing the Edges

Landscape contours should be cut from hardboard or thin ply. This is then bent to fit against the ends of the cross-members. The ends of the cross-members can be trimmed, if necessary, to allow for an even curve. The contours can then be screwed into the end of the cross-members.

If you wish to mount controls in the edge panels then these should be recessed so that they don't protrude and catch people as they pass by.

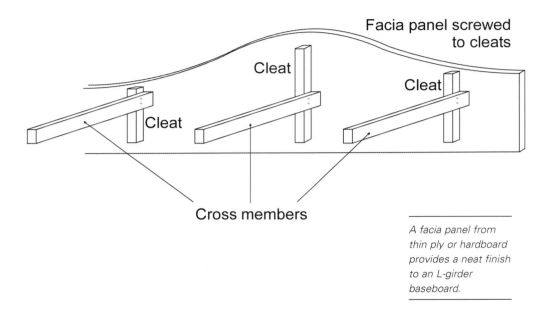

A facia panel from thin ply or hardboard provides a neat finish to an L-girder baseboard.

Plywood Beams and Other Materials

Whilst timber has been used for baseboard frames since the earliest days of railway modelling, over the years virtually every possible material has been tried as an alternative on the basis of cost, convenience, ease of construction, durability or just to see if it is usable. Even such unlikely candidates as cardboard boxes have provided the basis of model railways. Two materials that have become popular in recent years are plywood beams and foamcore board.

Plywood Beams

Plywood has long been used for the roadbed on model railways but is now a popular choice for the frame as well. The chief advantages are that the baseboard can be made lighter than a timber-framed equivalent and curved baseboards can be constructed with ease, freeing the layout builder from the usual straight lines and right-angle corners.

How two lengths of thin plywood become strong when joined together as an L- or T-girder.

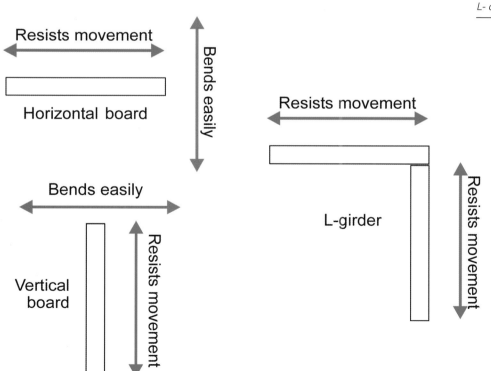

Ply strip from above - can bend easily to either side and twist end to end

Two lengths of ply joined together side by side make a strong and lightweight girder.

Two ply strips joined with spacers, seen from above.
If the top strip starts to bend upwards, the bottom strip holds it back as it resists being pulled longer. Similarly each strip resists the other strip being twisted. Result: a rigid girder.

When two lengths of relatively flimsy plywood are joined together they make a beam that is surprisingly resistant to bending. The methods used for model railway baseboards are to make the ply strips into an 'L' or 'T' shape or to use two lengths joined side by side.

You will need a lot of spacers so it pays to produce then in a batch rather than cut them as needed. Here 2" × 1" (50mm x 25mm) timber is being cut into 3" (75mm) lengths to use in 3" (75mm) deep girders.
Photo: Author's collection

Where two lengths are joined together it is normal to insert some spacers, either of timber or ply, to make the resulting girder a similar width to a length of timber, although much lighter and resistant to warping or bending. Such girders can be used as a direct replacement for timber when building any form of baseboard.

Ply beams used as a conventional frame for a solid-top baseboard.

The same baseboard seen from above. The railway is on an embankment along the back.

Baseboard Viewed From Underneath

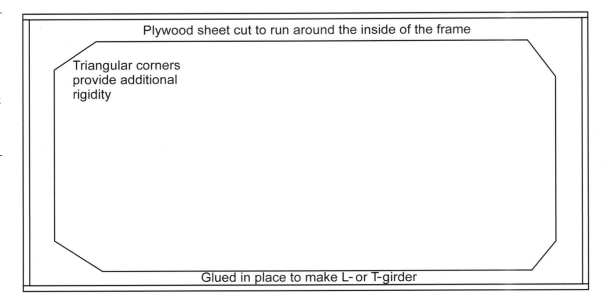

With a thin plywood outer frame and a strip of ply running round the inside at right-angles you can create a rigid T-girder. The extra wood at the corners helps to provide extra rigidity.

Plywood sheet cut to run around the inside of the frame

Triangular corners provide additional rigidity

Glued in place to make L- or T-girder

Outer frame made from plywood sheet

The baseboards for Tim Maddocks' Bleakhouse Road layout combine thin ply beams round the outside in a T-girder arrangement with an inner web cut from thicker plywood.
Photo: Tim Maddocks

The baseboard sides for Bleakhouse Road are made from two strips of 4mm plywood with 4mm ply spacers giving a 12mm wide girder that is exceedingly light and strong.
Photo: Tim Maddocks

Drilling holes in a plywood strip to reduce the weight

In order to reduce the weight of your baseboard even further it is possible to cut circles out of the plywood without reducing the strength of the girder too much. Use of a hole-cutter mounted in a power drill will make short work of the job.

Flush Doors

Modern flush doors can be used for baseboards, provided you can accommodate the size. Standard doors are 6'6" (197.6cm) × 2'6" (76cm) which could make a single piece baseboard for an 'N' scale layout. This type of door consists of two panels covering a frame. Unfortunately it is not possible to cut them down to provide smaller baseboards. Legs or other fixings need to be attached to the wood frame around the door.

As there are empty areas between the two skins it can be difficult to feed wires down through the baseboard. If you want to run wires under the baseboard it is best to line the holes for them with a drinking straw whilst you push the wire through. This will make sure that the wire goes through the board rather than inside it.

Foamcore Board

Foamcore board is a relatively recent material. It consists of a sheet of poly-styrene foam sandwiched between two layers of card. It comes in 5mm and 10mm thicknesses and is mainly used to make signs, especially the large ones that supermarkets suspend over your head. It has the advantage of being rigid but light. It is also possible to scrounge old signs from some businesses which gives it the added advantage of being free.

If you are unable to scrounge some it can be obtained from art and graphic supply shops in sizes ranging from A4 sheets up to A0 (that is about 46″ × 33″ or 118cm × 84cm – the total area being one square metre).

Foamcore board can be cut with a Stanley knife and a straight edge, glued with a hot glue gun and can replace plywood in I and T beams. Whilst foamcore board is strong and rigid when made into girders, it cannot be used to hold screws, alignment dowels or anything which would compress the board. Thus you need to use timber or plywood sections in places where you need to screw or bolt anything to the baseboard.

Foamcore board is better suited to frame-style open-top baseboards rather than the grid type (see chapter 4) as attaching risers to support the trackbed can be problematical. It is ideally suited to a solid-top baseboard, especially if you use foamcore as the baseboard surface. This gives you an exceedingly light baseboard which is easy to lift and carry.

Here some 5mm thick foamcore board salvaged from a supermarket sign has been used as bracing and some of the girders for these baseboards. Plywood has been used for the girders where the baseboards join and need alignment dowels and coach bolts to be fitted. Photo: Author's collection

Shelves

A length of shelving, such as ContiBoard can make a simple and effective baseboard for a small shunting layout. The board can either be part of a shelving system or just placed on a suitable surface such as a large table.

Wiring will need to be restricted to the top of the baseboard, and this type of system can be an excellent way of getting something running whilst you work on a larger layout.

Track can be temporarily fixed using double-sided sticky tape and a shunting puzzle-type layout, such as the 'Inglenook Sidings' one illustrated can be put together and operating in under an hour.

Given a run of bookcases along a wall it would be possible to build a terminus to fiddle yard layout. Alternatively a narrow layout could be run on shelf brackets around any suitable room, such as a spare bedroom or study.

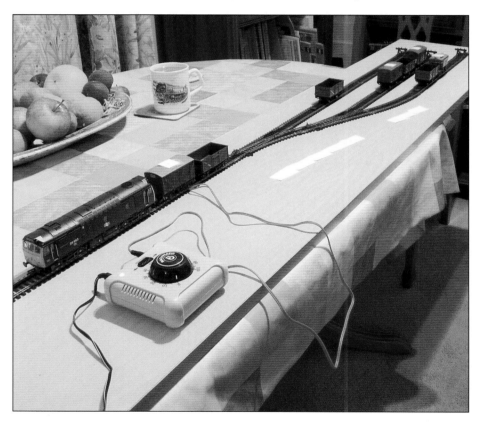

The classic 'Inglenook Sidings' shunting puzzle can be set up in under an hour on a length of shelving.
This is an ideal way to get something running while you work on a larger project.
Alternatively, if you are short of space, you can apply a full scenic treatment and use it as a complete layout.
Photo: Author's collection

Coffee Tables

Small layouts, typically in 'N' scale or '00' narrow gauge, can be built into glass-topped coffee tables. These not only make use of space that would be otherwise unavailable for modelling but make attractive features in themselves. Whilst the table could be built specially for the layout, it is easier to buy a suitable table from a shop such as Ikea and then design the layout to fit.

Jim Stanhope constructed this 'N' gauge layout in a specially built table that is 38" (97cm) long, 18" (46cm) wide and 14" (36cm) tall. The toughened glass panel measures 26" (66cm) by 14" (36cm).
Photo: Jim Stanhope

The layout is mounted on a detachable base under the table top for access and maintenance.
Photo: Jim Stanhope

Legs and Supports

Whatever type of baseboard you use, they all need some means of support to keep them off the floor. The subject of what the correct height is for a model railway has consumed many pages of magazines and caused much discussion amongst modellers. Some people like their layouts to give an eye-level view, others prefer something around a normal table-top height so that they can reach across the baseboard easily. No matter what height you decide on, the supports must be stable and capable of supporting the model.

You need to bear in mind that the higher a layout is from the ground the harder it is to reach across it or work on it. If you want a layout that gives an eye-level view you will be limited to a baseboard that is about as wide as your arm is long. Even then you will need to stand on something for some jobs, unless you can take the boards somewhere else to work on them. An alternative is to set the height so that it gives an eye-level view when you are sitting on a stool. That way you gain some extra width as you can bend over the layout. Often fixed obstructions in the layout's room such as radiators or windows limit the choice of heights.

The ideal baseboard height varies depending on a wide variety of factors, from location to personal preference.
These baseboards give an eye-level view of the layout. The need for a freezer to fit underneath one of the boards meant that a lower height was not possible.
Photo: Author's collection

Permanent Layouts

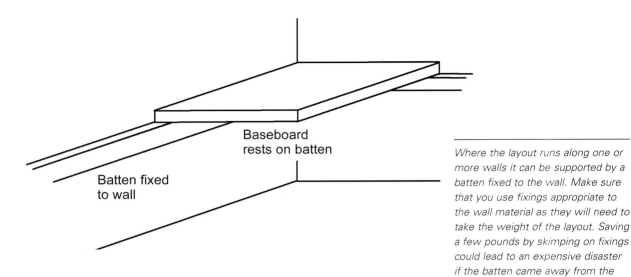

Baseboard
rests on batten

Batten fixed
to wall

Where the layout runs along one or more walls it can be supported by a batten fixed to the wall. Make sure that you use fixings appropriate to the wall material as they will need to take the weight of the layout. Saving a few pounds by skimping on fixings could lead to an expensive disaster if the batten came away from the wall with the layout in place.

Baseboard

Leg

Most layouts run along one or more walls and so it is convenient to secure those sides to the wall. It is best to run a batten along the wall for the baseboard to rest on rather than secure the baseboard direct to the wall. It is far easier to make the batten level than a number of baseboards where you will need to work from underneath with restricted access.

The front edge of the baseboard can be supported in a number of different ways. Timber legs are the usual means employed. These are typically of $2'' \times 1''$ (50mm $\times$ 25mm) or $2'' \times 2''$ (50mm $\times$ 50mm) which are screwed to the baseboard frame. For layouts that are unlikely to move it is possible to place a leg at the baseboard join.

By putting a recess into the top of the leg it can be positioned so that half of the width supports each baseboard. This acts as a built in levelling system for the baseboard join, ensuring that both baseboard tops are perfectly aligned.

For permanent or movable layouts legs can be screwed firmly in place. As a bonus they can also be used to join and align baseboards.

Bookcases

An alternative to legs is to use self-assembly bookcase units but this can restrict access to the underside of the baseboards. It is best to make limited use of these, ensuring that there is still room to get at the wiring. In my opinion it would make an ideal system for supporting a 5′ × 3′ (152cm × 91cm) or 6′ × 4′ (182cm × 121cm) layout in a child's room as it would provide useful storage space.

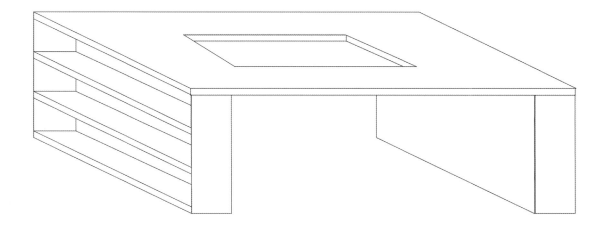

Self-assembly bookcases come in a variety of sizes and are readily available. You can use one or more as layout supports with the added benefit of some useful storage space.

Folding Legs

Portable and movable layouts require a different approach. With this type of baseboard the legs need to be easily transportable. The two common solutions are to use legs that fold into the baseboard or separate trestles.

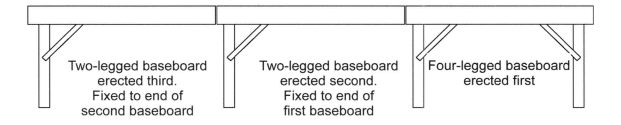

Two-legged baseboard erected third. Fixed to end of second baseboard

Two-legged baseboard erected second. Fixed to end of first baseboard

Four-legged baseboard erected first

With folding legs common practice is for one baseboard to have four legs, one at each corner and for the other baseboards to have only two. The four-legged baseboard is erected first and then the other baseboards are joined to it, the legless end of each baseboard being supported by its neighbour. This technique is known as 'piggy-back'. Whilst it does minimise the number of legs that are needed, only the board with four legs is capable of being erected on its own. This can be a disadvantage when you wish to work on one of the two-legged boards without erecting the whole layout.

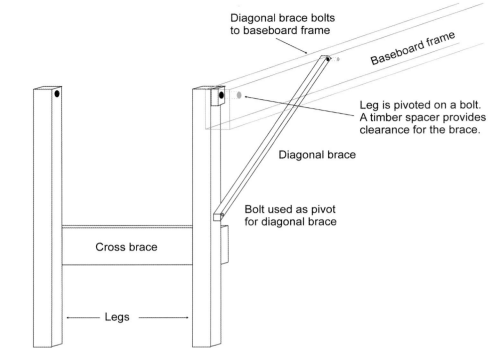

Diagonal brace bolts
to baseboard frame

Baseboard frame

Leg is pivoted on a bolt.
A timber spacer provides
clearance for the brace.

Diagonal brace

Bolt used as pivot
for diagonal brace

Cross brace

Legs

*Folding legs need
some form of brace
to keep them in
place. This is usually
a length of thin
timber that bolts to
the baseboard
frame.*
*A second length of
timber or plywood
acts as a cross brace
to give stability
across the layout.*

The folding legs need a diagonal brace to keep them in position when they are folded down. This is usually a length of timber that either bolts to the baseboard structure or uses a hinge to fix into place. The two legs of each pair also need some form of cross bracing, usually a strip of plywood or timber, to keep them aligned. The legs can either be hinged to the baseboard end or use a bolt that passes through both the leg and the baseboard side as a pivot.

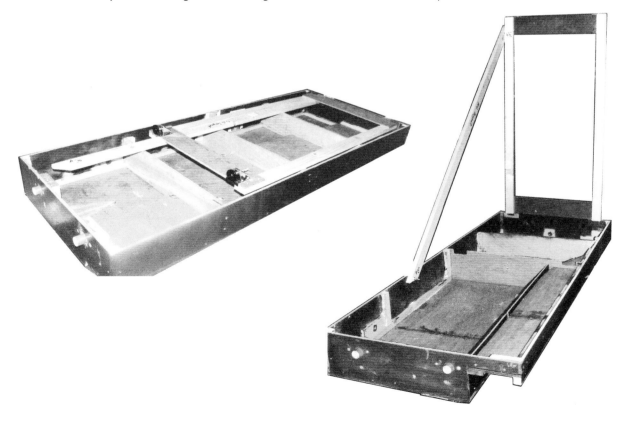

A portable baseboard that has a pair of hinged legs built in. The timber legs are cross-braced both at the top and bottom with plywood strips. The diagonal brace is a further length of timber that bolts to the baseboard frame.

This baseboard has only one pair of legs and is designed to 'piggy-back' off another board.

The legs fold down inside the baseboard frame for transport. The diagonal brace also stows away inside the frame.

This baseboard has two pairs of legs and is the first to be erected. The other baseboards have only one pair of legs each and 'piggy-back' off this board.

One problem that affects all portable and movable layouts is uneven floors. It is very rare to find a floor that is both flat and level and, as a result, however carefully you have cut and fitted your baseboard legs they won't all touch the floor at once. To solve this it will be necessary to adjust the height of one or more legs to get a layout that is level, flat and does not rock.

The simplest way to level a layout is to insert thin pieces of plywood under the legs to even things up. The disadvantage of this is that it is difficult to get things spot-on and it is easy for some of the pieces to get dislodged. A far better solution is to build in some measure of adjustability when constructing the legs.

One method is to drill a hole in the bottom of the leg, mount a pronged tee nut over the hole and use a bolt as an adjustable foot. If you use a hexagonal headed bolt then you will be able to adjust each leg using a spanner to get them set to give a perfectly level layout. Unfortunately this does require that you use substantial timber, at least 2" × 2" (50mm × 50mm) for your legs and you have to drill the hole into the end grain of the wood – its weakest part.

An alternative is to purchase adjustable feet that consist of a metal bracket that screws to the side of the leg. The foot can be screwed up or down and also swivels so that it sits firmly on the floor.

Trestles

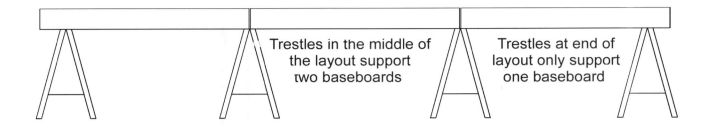

Trestles in the middle of the layout support two baseboards

Trestles at end of layout only support one baseboard

Trestles can either be purchased ready-made from places like Ikea and DIY stores, or made from hinges and timber. Each trestle is free-standing and at least two will be needed. Where a layout consists of a number of baseboards it is normal to have a trestle under each baseboard joint.

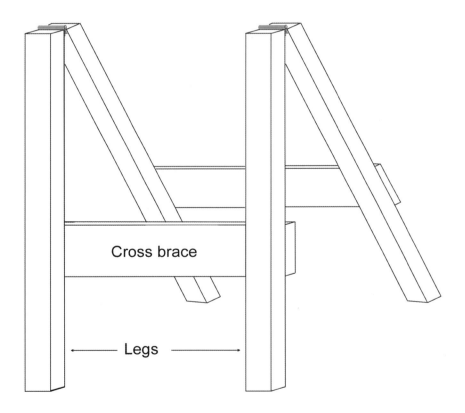

Cross brace

←——— Legs ———→

Each trestle consists of two pairs of legs that are hinged together. Some means of stopping them moving apart needs to be provided. This can be as simple as a piece of string or a brace that bolts in place.

Separate Supports

Iain Rice devised a system where the supporting structure is separate from the layout itself. Thus the supports can be used for a number of different layouts. This system allows you to have two, or more, portable layouts that can use the same legs. This may seem an odd idea at first, but many modellers find that their interests encompass different scales, companies or even countries. By having, for example, an 'HO' scale US shunting layout and a Great Western branch terminus a modeller can switch between the two at whim. The layout and stock that are not in use can be stored away until they are needed again.

   Another benefit of this system is that it can serve many layouts over the years. A lot of people regularly build new layouts and have to invest time and money in providing new supports for each one. The separate support system is flexible and can be adapted as a layout grows, changes or is replaced.

Here a separate support structure is being used to support a baseboard for an 'N' gauge layout (shown in chapter 3) and a section of an 'OO' gauge layout under construction.
Photo: Author's collection

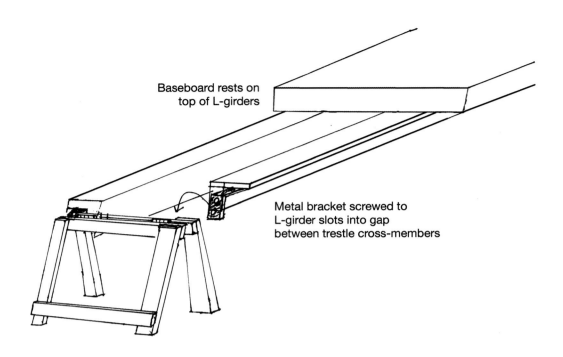

Baseboard rests on
top of L-girders

Metal bracket screwed to
L-girder slots into gap
between trestle cross-members

The basis of the system is a pair of L-girders which run the length of the layout site. Depending on your baseboard type you may wish to add cross-members to support the baseboards. The L-girders are cut down to manageable lengths of around 5' to 6' (1.5m to 1.8m) with fixed legs or trestles between them.

Steel right-angle brackets are screwed to the ends of the L-girders and these locate between the cross-members at the top of the trestles. The trestle hinges make a gap between the cross-members that is just the right size for the brackets to fit in.

A section of Kier Hardy's portable exhibition layout Wibdenshaw.
Photo: Kier Hardy

Joining and Aligning

CHAPTER

Whenever you have a layout that is spread over two or more baseboards you have the problem of joining and aligning them. Good and consistent alignment is crucial to ensure that you don't experience derailments as trains cross from one baseboard to the next and that the scenery doesn't have large gaps or trenches in it.

Obviously, if you have decided that the layout is never going to be moved then you can simply screw the baseboard sections together and treat the resulting structure as a single unit. However, if you want to be able to move the layout or take individual baseboards off the layout to work on them then you need some means of ensuring that they fit back in the right place.

The traditional methods of joining baseboards are to use hinges and/or coach bolts. More recently the use of cabinet makers' and pattern makers' dowels has become popular to ensure accurate alignment, chiefly due to the smaller scales and finer tolerances that have appeared over the years. Many other schemes of varying degrees of ingenuity have been devised and implemented over the years but they haven't received widespread acceptance.

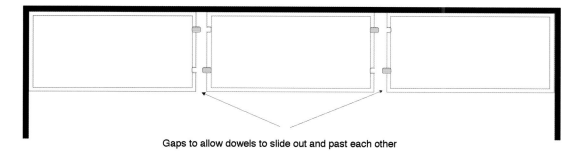

Gaps to allow dowels to slide out and past each other

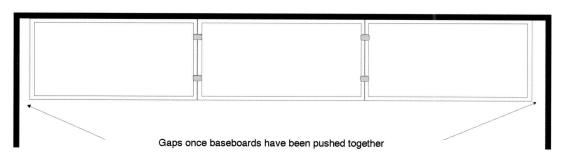

Gaps once baseboards have been pushed together

Allow a little space around the layout so that it is possible to get the baseboards in and out easily. This will allow you to remove a single baseboard to work on or even replace.

One aspect that is often overlooked is that dowels need a small gap between the baseboards when they are being taken apart. This can catch you out if you are trying to squeeze every last inch of layout into the space available. In this case you will have to use one of the alternative systems. However, if your layout is portable or movable the few spare inches lost to make space for the dowels is a good trade-off against trying to slide a tight-fitting baseboard out from the layout.

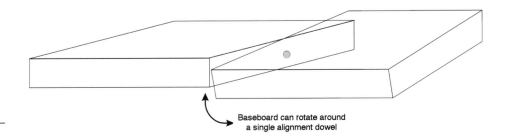

Baseboard can rotate around
a single alignment dowel

*Always use two
location dowels
between
baseboards. If you
use only one the
baseboards will be
able to move out of
alignment.*

You will normally need two alignment devices, be they dowels, hinges or spring catches, between each pair of baseboards. If you use only one dowel the baseboards can move out of alignment by rotating around the dowel. On a wide baseboard you may find it useful to use three dowels, but given a rigid structure this should not normally be necessary. If the alignment devices don't secure the baseboards you will also need one or more bolts or catches to keep the baseboards together.

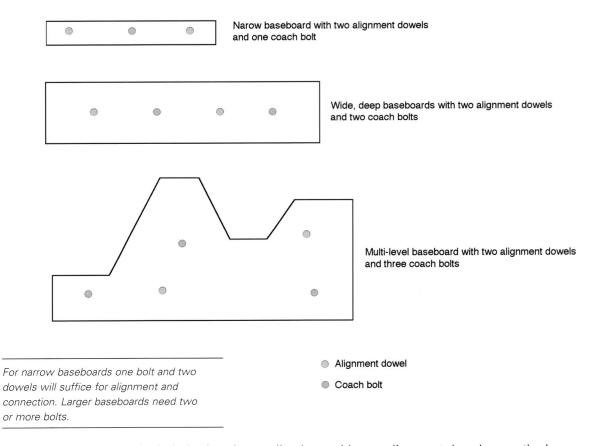

Narow baseboard with two alignment dowels
and one coach bolt

Wide, deep baseboards with two alignment dowels
and two coach bolts

Multi-level baseboard with two alignment dowels
and three coach bolts

◯ Alignment dowel

◯ Coach bolt

*For narrow baseboards one bolt and two
dowels will suffice for alignment and
connection. Larger baseboards need two
or more bolts.*

A single bolt placed centrally along with two alignment dowels near the baseboard edges should be sufficient for most purposes. Some people prefer to have two bolts to avoid the possibility of any gaps opening up if the baseboards flex.

Coach Bolts

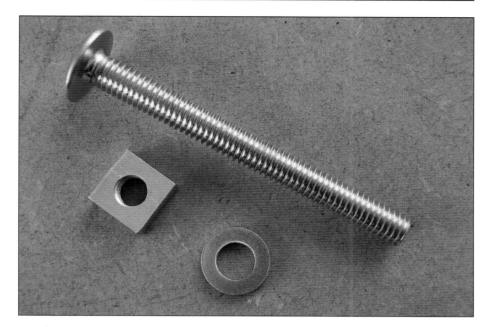

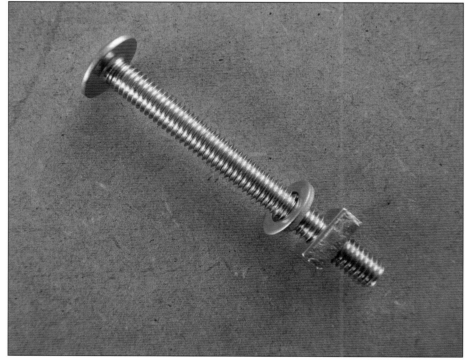

Coach bolts come with a variety of head styles. The nuts can be square, hexagonal or wing. Wing nuts are easy to tighten by hand. Always use a washer between the baseboard and the nut to stop it being pulled into the wood.

The long coach bolt has been used to join baseboards for many years. Originally it was used to provide both strength and alignment. Unfortunately regular removal and insertion causes the hole in the baseboard to wear, leading to alignment problems. Current practice is to use coach bolts to hold baseboards together whilst dowels provide the accurate alignment.

Coach bolts come with a variety of heads: the one illustrated is domed, others can be hexagonal so that they can be held with a spanner, or circular and slotted for a screwdriver. Similarly, a variety of nuts can be used: square, hexagonal or wing nuts which are easier for tightening by hand.

A washer between the baseboard and the nut will help to stop the nut digging into the wood of the baseboard frame.

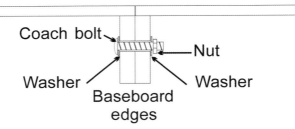

To install coach bolts you need to select a bolt that is roughly three times as long as the baseboard end member is thick. Thus for a baseboard with an 18mm thick end timber you would need a bolt around 60mm long. It needs to be long enough to pass through both baseboard ends, a nut and a washer and still have a little thread showing. Clamp the two baseboards together and drill a hole just larger than the diameter of the bolt through the baseboard ends. The bolt should be a sliding fit in the hole rather than needing to be screwed in. You will normally need two bolts for each join to avoid any unwanted movement. Particularly wide baseboards may need more bolts.

*A hexagonal headed
coach bolt with
pronged tee nuts.
The nuts fix
themselves into the
baseboard frame. No
washers are needed
and there are fewer
parts to keep track of
when you take the
baseboards apart.*

A refinement on the coach bolt technique is to use pronged tee nuts. These stop the bolt from wearing the wood away and avoid the need for a separate nut. One of the tee nuts is a sliding fit on the bolt; the other has threads and replaces the nut. The prongs dig into the wood and hold the tee nut in place.

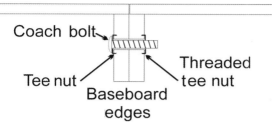

Use of a sliding tee nut on the bolt side means that the bolt has only to be screwed into the nut on the other baseboard. If both nuts are threaded it can be difficult to fit the bolt.

To fit them you need to drill the hole for the bolt as a clearance hole for the tube section of the tee nut. Place the sliding tee nut over the bolt and push the bolt through the hole. Screw the threaded tee nut onto the bolt and tighten until both the nuts have dug into the wood and are held firm. If you smear a little contact adhesive, such as Evo-Stick, on the side of the nut that lies against the wood before you tighten it up then there is no danger of the nut working loose over time.

Hinges

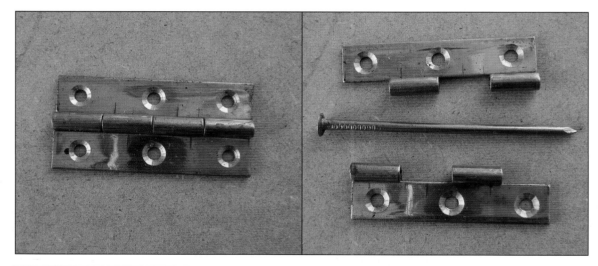

Brass hinges are a tried and trusted method of aligning and joining baseboards. Whilst the system is simple it is remarkably effective.

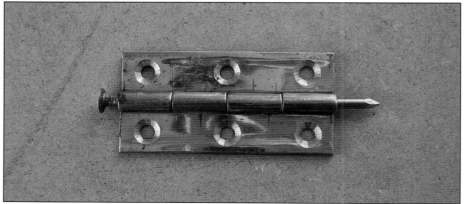

One of the oldest methods for joining and aligning baseboards and still popular today is to use a brass hinge. Screw one side of the hinge to one baseboard, and the other to the other. Using a suitable nail knock the pin out of the hinge and replace the pin with either a nail or a length of metal rod.

The baseboards joined together with the hinge pin in place.

The baseboards separated. Bending the pin ensures that it will not slip through the hinge and fall out. It also makes it easier to use.

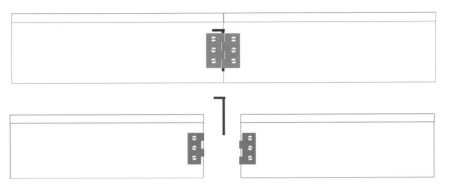

To separate the baseboards, take the new pin out. To fix them together line up both halves of the hinge and insert the new pin.

Spring Catches

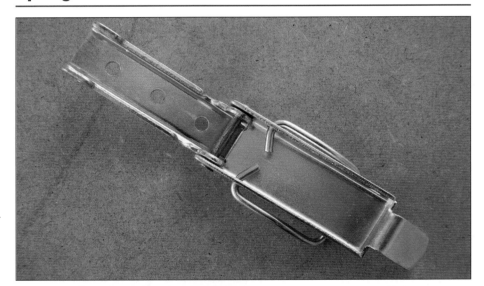

Spring catches are very quick to use. Another advantage for portable layouts is that they are self-contained with no parts that can be mislaid.

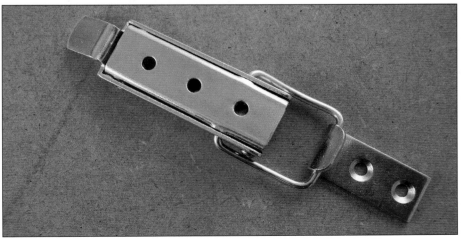

A fairly recent addition to the railway modeller's armoury is the spring catch. Whilst these can provide both mechanical strength and alignment it is normal to use them in conjunction with dowels.

The great advantage of spring catches is the speed of use, enabling a portable layout to be set up remarkably quickly. The disadvantages are that they are only suitable for joining baseboards that have straight edges and where both sides are accessible. You can't use them underneath a baseboard or on a layout that has one side against a wall.

Installation is simple. Clamp the two baseboards together, hold the catch in position and mark the screw holes. Open the holes out with a pilot drill and then screw both parts of the catch in place.

Cabinet Makers' Dowels

Cabinet makers' dowels are simple to install and align baseboards accurately. However, you do need to provide some means of securing the baseboards so that they don't come apart.

These devices come in pairs of a male plug and a female socket. They provide accurate alignment to an accuracy of about 0.005" (0.0125mm). They do not provide any means of holding the baseboards together, only aligning them.

To fit them you need to drill a hole in the baseboard ends. This is easier to do before you assemble the baseboard as both timbers can be clamped together and drilled on your workbench. If you need to fit the dowels in situ then take extra care to check that the holes align properly.

The first step is to drill a pilot hole of around 1/8" (2–3mm) diameter to act as a guide. The pilot hole will help to guide the larger drill and ensure that it does not wander and cut over-size. For an 8mm outside diameter dowel you will then need to open the hole out with a 9/32" (7.5mm) drill.

Now press the male half in using finger pressure and then place the female half over it whilst you lightly tap it home with a hammer. Place the female half into the corresponding hole on the other baseboard, press it in place and then lightly tap home with the hammer.

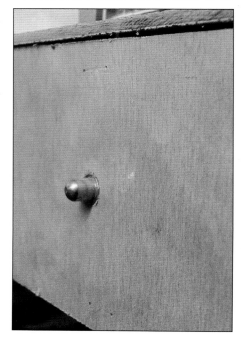

A male dowel installed on a plywood baseboard end. You can either install two males on one board and two females on the other or a male and female on each.

Bring the two boards together to check the alignment. If necessary a light tap with the hammer on the male dowel or the baseboard top will serve to make the join level.

If the male dowel is knocked out of alignment at any time, usually caused by the baseboard end hitting, or being hit by, something, a gentle tap with a hammer should realign it.

Pattern Makers' Dowels

Pattern makers' dowels provide a high level of accuracy. This is ideal if you require absolute precision at your baseboard joins, for example where you are using P4 or 2mm finescale track.

These are the de luxe solution to the problem of aligning baseboards. Typically they align with an accuracy of 0.002" (0.005mm). Again, they do not provide any means of holding the baseboards together.

They are harder to fit than cabinet makers' dowels. To fit them you need to drill a hole in the baseboard ends. This is easier to do before you assemble the baseboard as both timbers can be clamped together and drilled on your workbench. If you need to fit the dowels in situ then take extra care to check that the holes align properly.

The dowels illustrated have a flange 1/8" (3mm) thick and 1" (25mm) diameter. The spigot is 7/16" (10mm) long with a diameter of 0.31" (7.75mm). The first step is to drill a pilot hole of around 1/8" (2–3mm) diameter to act as a guide. The pilot hole will help to guide the larger drill and ensure that it does not wander and cut over-size. Separate the boards and drill a 1" diameter 1/8" deep hole on both boards. Next, you need to drill a 10mm deep, 8mm diameter hole on the side that will be fitted with the female section. This hole is where the spigot will fit when the boards are aligned. Put the dowels in the holes and then screw them in place.

No further fixing, such as glue, is required and nothing will cause them to move out of alignment short of major damage to the baseboard.

Once the track and basic groundwork is in place the baseboards start to look like a model railway. This is Tim Maddocks' Bleakhouse Road, an 'OO' scale exhibition layout based on a station in Somerset. The two scenic boards, shown here, each measure four feet long by twenty-two inches wide (that's about 122cm x 55cm). Each board has a pair of folding legs fitted to the outer ends. A folding trestle supports the baseboard join. This method allows the baseboards to be erected either as a pair or individually. **Photo: Tim Maddocks**

CHAPTER

Portability

any people believe that the only reason to make a layout portable is so
that it can be taken to model railway exhibitions. A little thought will,
however, indicate that there are other potential benefits of a portable layout.
For those of us who have to move about a lot, either due to work or studies,
a portable layout is an ideal solution to life in bed-sit land. Similarly those
who are settled but cannot find anywhere to house a permanent layout could
also benefit from an easy to store and quick to erect model railway. A portable
layout could also be used as a little 'light relief' from a larger layout: for
example a US-outline switching layout to contrast with the East Coast Main
Line in the loft.

There is a difference between a movable layout and a portable one. Any
layout that can be broken down into sections without damage can be classed as
movable. This does not necessarily mean that they are suitable for regular
erection and disassembly. A portable layout needs to be designed so that when
it is in its disassembled state it is reasonably well protected from damage.
Reassembly should be relatively quick and easy. Most important, the layout
should be easy to move without damage to the layout, the building or the
owner.

Portable layouts may be designed to sit on suitable items of furniture, such
as bookcases and tables, fit on collapsible trestles or have built-in legs. Some
have special packing cases that they slide into, some have special boxes, others
are bolted together with the backscene helping to protect the model. There is no
end to the number of different ways that people have devised to convert sections
of layout into easily moved items. The one thing that you do not want to do is try
to move and store unprotected baseboards on a regular basis. Sooner rather
than later they will be knocked, dropped or caught on a doorway, ruining hours
of work.

This is a small folding layout that was built by the late Mike Pearson and Steve Best of Hull Miniature Railway Society. The basic structure consists of two timber frame solid-top baseboards that are hinged together. In the closed position two struts are bolted to the outside ends of the boards to make a box with the scenic section on the inside.
Photo: Neil Ripley

Another consideration that must be taken into account is how many of the scenic items will be fixed down and how many will be removable. The more items that have to be put in place each time the layout is erected and then removed before it can be taken down, the more of a chore the task will become and the more likely that some will be forgotten until they fall off the layout.

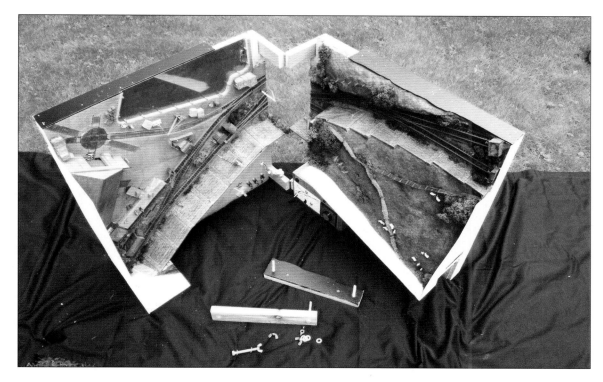

Once the end struts have been unbolted the two boards can be swung open. The hinges are on struts so that there is sufficient clearance for the scenery when the layout is folded up. As you can see, all the buildings and scenic accessories are firmly fixed in place. This ensures that they don't get lost or damaged when the layout is set up and taken down.
Photo: Neil Ripley

The layout is now in the fully open position. When set up the layout measures 4' × 2' (121.6cm × 60.8cm). In its folded state it makes a box measuring 2' × 2' × 16" (60.8cm × 60.8cm × 20.3cm). The controls are built into the baseboard.
Photo: Neil Ripley

The front hinge is mounted on dowels so that it can be hinged down and hidden with a removable building. If the hinges are fixed in position they can still be disguised with removable scenery.
Photo: Neil Ripley

A length of wood with a section of facia is bolted in place over the hinge to hold the layout rigidly in the open position and provide a continuous facia at the front.
Photo: Neil Ripley

With the facia in place and the removable building covering the hinge area the front of the layout is complete. The track is standard 'OO' gauge Peco Setrack, although some pieces were cut to fit.
Photo: Neil Ripley

This is the view from behind the layout. The rear hinge is fixed in the upright position as there is no benefit in making it fold down. The traverser to the right is simply a piece of plywood with a screw at the right-hand end which acts as a pivot. The traverser simply slides on the top of the solid baseboard. The tracks are all laid on plywood attached to the baseboard top. A simple sliding wire loop pushes into tubes to align the traverser with the three exit tracks. The electrical feeds for the traverser are soldered directly to the rails at the pivot end.
Photo: Neil Ripley

A multi-way electrical plug provides electrical connections between the two boards. It can be seen here plugged into the control box. A piece of removable scenery is used to fill the remaining gap along the retaining wall.
Photo: Neil Ripley

Here is the completed layout ready for use. In this form it could be used on a large table. In its folded form the layout was designed to be stored in the bottom of a wardrobe.
Photo: Neil Ripley

A set of legs with wooden cross members allows the layout to be free-standing. The folding black arms are for mounting an overhead facia board. This combined with a curtain around the layout's base provides a full exhibition-style layout.
Photo: Neil Ripley

Apart from the rolling stock everything you see here is firmly fixed down, allowing the layout to be erected and dismantled quickly.
Photo: Neil Ripley

At the other end of the scale are layouts like Kier Hardy's Wibdenshaw. Whilst this layout was designed to be taken to exhibitions it does require a lot of work from a team of people to transport and erect it.
Photo: Kier Hardy

The fiddle yard on Wibdenshaw has been cleverly designed so that it can be moved with the rolling stock in place, not only saving a great deal of time when erecting and dismantling the layout but also ensuring that none of the stock is forgotten.
Photo: Kier Hardy

Here is the fiddle yard section of Wibdenshaw neatly packed. Note that all the boards and packing pieces are clearly marked to avoid confusion.
Photo: Kier Hardy

Portable Layouts – Some things to consider	
Overall finish	As the layout will, in all likelihood, either be in a well-used room or on public display take time to finish off the baseboard edges and supports neatly. Bare wood and jagged edges are best left to layouts that are in their own room.
Need to be lightweight	Consider smaller baseboards or a lightweight construction method such as plywood or foamcore board. If it needs two people to move a baseboard, will you always be able to find someone to help when needed?
Need some form of support	Built-in legs mean that there are no extra pieces to move (or forget). Collapsible trestles allow baseboards to be set up individually so that you can work on them. Trestles and separate support systems can be used for a number of different layouts.
Need some form of alignment	Don't rely on coach bolts in holes to align your baseboards and track accurately. As the holes wear the alignment gets worse. The baseboards and tracks need to align consistently and accurately every time the layout is assembled.
Need some form of vertical alignment	Vertical alignment needs to be adjustable, either by an adjustable foot on each leg or the simple expedient of packing legs with scrap material.
Need to be protected when disassembled	Make baseboards in pairs that can be bolted together face to face or hinge together. Use the backscene as part of the protective covering.
Need reliable electrical connections	Consider minimising the number of wires needed by using DCC rather than conventional control. Consider manual operation of points and signals.
Need safe electrics and cabling	Don't leave hanging wires or cables that might get caught up on things. If you need to use a trailing mains cable make sure that it won't cause a tripping hazard – apart from the obvious danger of injury, the falling victim might take the layout with them.
Need secure stock boxes	Make sure that the rolling stock is safe and secure when transported. Either use the manufacturer's original packaging or other suitable containers. If you leave stock free to roll around, it will.
Things need to be fixed down	Anything that is not firmly fixed in place must be taken off the layout, safely packed, transported and replaced on the layout every time it is moved. The fewer items that need individual treatment, the better.
Label things clearly	Clear labelling will save time and avoid confusion by making sure that the right part goes in the right place.
Checklist	Have a checklist for taking the layout down, and another for putting it back together. That way you can make sure that you remember all the bits and pieces and do things in the right order.

Appendix – Useful Addresses

All Components
Baseboard fittings such as pattern makers' dowels, adjustable feet and spring catches.
PO Box 94, Hereford, HR2 8YN
Tel: 01981 540781
www.allcomponents.co.uk
Mail order only. Not open to callers.

B & R Model Railways
Baseboards made to order. Based near Hull.
77 Darvell Drive, Chesham, HP5 2QN (correspondence address only)
Tel: 01494 783988
www.bandrmodelrailways.co.uk

Black Cat Baseboards
Baseboards made to order. Based near Hull.
Contact via email either on colin@clastark.karoo.co.uk or info@blackcatbaseboards.co.uk
www.blackcatbaseboards.co.uk

Carrs – C+L Finescale
Baseboard fittings such as pattern makers' dowels, adjustable feet, pronged tee nuts.
c/o LCP International Ltd,
Longridge House, Cadbury Camp Lane, Clapton in Gordano, Bristol, BS20 7SD
Tel: 01275 852027
www.finescale.org.uk

Jewson
National chain of builders' merchants with 450 branches.
Branch locator available on their website.
Tel: 0800 539766
www.jewson.co.uk

Scalecraft
Baseboards made to order.
Silver Oaks Farm, Waldron, East Sussex, TN21 0RS
Tel: 01273 812023
www.scalecraft.co.uk

Sundeala Limited
Manufacturer of Sundeala board. Contact them for details of local suppliers.
Middle Mill, Cam, Dursley, GL11 5LQ
Tel: 01453 540900
www.sundeala.co.uk

Tay Bridge Models
Baseboards made to order. Not open to callers.
37 Finlarig Terrace, Dundee, Scotland, DD4 9JF
Tel: 01382 502584
www.taybridgemodels.co.uk

White Rose Modelworks
Baseboards made to order.
Unit 10, Bedale Station, The Bridge, Bedale, DL8 1BZ
Tel: 01677 422444

Yorkshire Woodcraft
Baseboards made to order.
276 High Street, Northallerton, Yorkshire, DL7 8DW
Tel: 01609 777214

HORNBY magazine

The best hands-on magazine for modellers of all ages

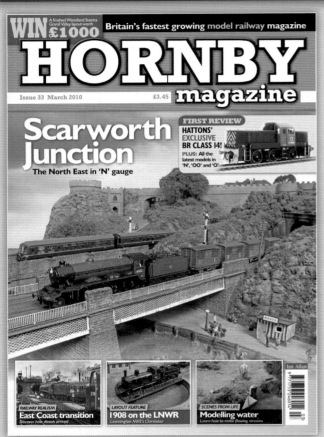

■ Step-by-step illustrated guidelines

■ Specially commissioned artwork

■ Artist's impressions and trackplans

■ Inspirational features supported by high quality photogra[phy]

■ Clear instructions on how to create your own models

■ Useful guidance on which products to use

■ Independent coverage of all new product releases

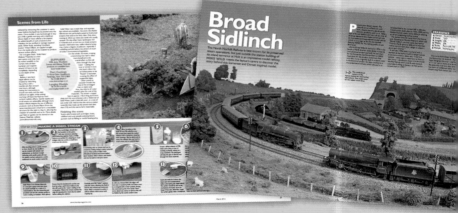

Keep up to date with all things modelling with a monthly subscription to Hornby Magazine!

GREAT SUBSCRIBER BENEFITS

■ Subscribe by quarterly Direct Debit

■ Receive each issue 'hot off the press' before the shops

■ Convenient home delivery so that you never miss an issue

■ FREE membership to the Ian Allan Publishing Subs Club

■ FREE personalised Subscription Loyalty Card

■ Exclusive access to new online site with great subscriber benefits, offers, and competitions. **Visit www.ianallanmagazines.com/subsclub for more details**

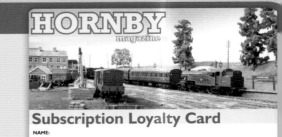

Subscription Loyalty Card

NAME:

MEMBERSHIP NO: EXPIRY DATE:

Subscribe online at www.hornbymagazine.com/subscribe or call +44(0)1932 266622. Also available to buy from all leading newsagent[s]